Heartfelt Expressions

Claudia Inglis

Olympus Story House

CONTENTS

ACKNOWLEDGEMENT

I give glory and honor to God my Father who has inspired me in all aspects of my life; and in every situation especially when everything was going rough.

Bibles used: NKJ, NLT, KJV, NSV for permission of scriptures and quotations used.

To my mother who did not know about my writing, but encouraged me; by telling me God has greater things for me to do; before she passed away and went to meet her Maker.

To my children Jillian, Nicole, and Shaun who are the joys of my life.

My friends Sylvia and Eric, who has been a great support and helped me with my family in critical situations.

Mother Banks who gave counsel and support when I lost my mom and encouraged me to write.

Sandra and Shariff Sr who were there in testing times. Sis turner helped with my editing.

Sis Griggs always been supportive and encouraging me. Professor Owens who had faith in me and saw my potential

Bro. Ronald and Bro Frankie my brothers in Christ who attended church with me; they encouraged me to read poems at programs; etching me on to pursue my writing.

To all God's children who has been supportive to me spiritually in this endeavor.

CHRISTIAN UNITY

Though we are from different parts of the globe
We are joined together by love
To work for the good of the Lord To help maintain our
Fathers' home Without any hardship,
Where we are able to meet for worship
We come together in unity
Through our Lord Jesus Christ the Divinity
To strengthen and uphold humanity
In our areas of Christianity
For the good of our community
The islands have seen it, and feared
The ends of the earth tremble
They approach and come forward
Each helps the other and says to his brother
Be strong, be strong

So do not fear for I am with you
Do not be dismayed for I am your God
I will strengthen you and help you
Isaiah 41:5-6

Now therefore ye are no more strangers and foreigners
But fellow citizens with the saints and of the household of God
Ephesians 2:19

PATIENCE

Patience is kind
Patience is pure
Patience is gentle
Makes you feel secure

Patience is humble
Patience is love
Patience is caring
Makes you endure

Patience is serene
Patience is not mean
Patience is going beyond
That which we have seen

Patience is good
Patience is faithful
Patience is beyond
All our knowledge and understanding;
We just have to be thankful and grateful;
For patience we know, comes straight from the heart.

A CHILD'S PLEA

Mother! Why do you weep?
Why do you moan?
I heard you pray,
I heard you groan.
Down on bended knees
There you've always been,
Knowing Gods' comfort is quite near.

The Lord, your keeper, your guide
With outstretched hands,
He helped you up,
He cradled and embraced you,
He came to lift your heavy burden,
He came to give you comfort, peace and joy.

He came so that you can be fulfilled,
By the Word and be spiritually edified.
Mother you do not have to weep or moan,
For the Lord He heard your prayer, your groan.

FATHER I STRETCH MY HANDS TO YOU

Father I stretch my hands to You,
No other help I know
When all around is sinking sand
You are the only one I know,
For helpless yet though I may be,
You are the Rock to which I can cleave
For my hope is in nothing else,
But in you, oh Lord! In you!

Why should I worry?
Why should I fear?
Though disaster and turmoil lingers near
For the Master He came
Not for His gain,
But to save us from sin and pain,.
He knows our joy and our sorrow,
He knows our today and tomorrow,
For in us He will abide,
If only we will not hide,
Always keeping open the door to our hearts,
So the Master, He will be able to come and reside.

We do not have to worry,
About what we do not know,
For if only we will allow Him,
His will shall be done

For in us He has invested,
So His Word and works can be manifested.
If we will surely acknowledge
And recognize His presence
Knowing that only He is priority in our life
He will cleanse us, he will elevate us,
He will ignite us, He will anoint us,
He will bless us,
Call on Him, He will answer.
Know that He is always near,
Take heed, He said every man is worthy in His sight.

He is a rewarder, of those who diligently seek Him
For if we commit our works unto Him
Then our thoughts shall be established,
He is our teacher, our preacher, our guide.

TRANQUILITY

Tranquility is the river of peace,
It gently flows from our hearts,
When we are calm and serene,
Blocking out all devastation and turmoil,
When the storm in our life rages,
Replacing peace in our haven;
Where we hibernate
And in the realm of our understanding,
Hope, joy, and love.

LOOK UP

I get up from my bed
Looking up towards the ceiling,
There above my head
Lay sheets of white with ridges.
Where am I?
What is going on?
Why oh why,
Am I distraught and perturbed?
I wonder, I ponder,
Though I drugged not,
But drank a great deal,
When I partied from dusk to dawn,
My good Lord He kept me from all harm.
I know I am a child of The Blessed One,
Who took a turn to follow the righteous way;
Why am I under such duress?
Knowing that Gods' grace and mercy covers me.
I then look up to the hills,
Where my help comes from
And remember Jesus' love for me,
Why He died on the cross at Calvary.
Then I no longer ask
Where, what and why?
But gently get down on my knees,
Into prayer and meditation,
Just thanking God for saving me.

PROVISION

I sit here and worry,
I wonder, I ponder,
I ask Lord, what do I do?
And where do I go?
There are bills to be paid,
The collectors are calling.
I hear the phone ringing.
Have fear of answering.
I begin to scream and shout,
My Lord, my God,
Who can this be?
Please help me out!
Why should I fear?
And wonder who's calling,
When I can sit here and ponder
With a bible in my hand,
The words the Lord has given
And provided for me,
That encouraged and strengthened.
He is the Rock on which I can stand.
He gave me faith so I can move mountains,
If I will only accept and acknowledge
The key He gave from above.
For it is in the Bible,
The Book of Love.

HE IS ALWAYS NEAR

In distress I call on the Lord.
In joy, I fail,
To call on Him,
He who is giver of life!
He is meek and humble,
He is always near
To give me assurance,
When I am in despair
He delivers me.
When I am sinking in sin;
He encamps around me.
When I am mentally drained;
He lifts my spirit.
When I am in distress;
He picks me up from the valley low,
When I do not know,
The way I should go.

HEALING

When I was sick
In a bed with affliction;
My Savior He took my hand in His hand.
He covered me with His precious blood.
I claimed with my voice,
The words with conviction,
"For by His stripes I know I am healed."
My Jesus He means the world to me,
For without Him,
Where would I be?
As I call on His names,
They strengthen me.
Jehovah Nissi the Lord my banner.
Adonai who is the Lord, My Great God;
Jehovah Rapha the Lord who heals.
Jehovah Shalom the Lord is Peace.
Jehovah Rohi the Lord is my Shepherd.
El The Strong One as He is called,
He is my precious Father from above.

HE KNOWS YOU

The Lord knows you,
He will help you.
He is always there for you;
When you are going through
He knew you from the start;
Because He made your heart

He only wants to hear
Your precious voice.;
Whispering softly; calling on Him.
Remember to call on
Him always In joy or in distress
Not your brother, sister or friend;
Only the Father from above!

On bended knees fervently pray,
Calling on Him unceasingly;
He will undoubtedly be there.
He will listen to you;
With His love and care

Yes! The Lord
He knows you,
He is the One who made your heart.
He knew you from your mother's womb,
He covered you with His precious blood,
He is Alpha, Omega, the beginning and the end.

ATTITUDE

Put away negativity,
By rejecting slander, confusion, conflict;
Continue to think positive, be more assertive,
Be spiritually inclined,
By releasing the humanistic thoughts;
When reproached, or provoked
Put on a spiritual robe;
In other words, be Christ like,
In whatever you do,
With love, caring, compassion,
Understanding and kindness,
The Lord our Father
Who sees and knows all,
Will surely reward you,
Who follow His steps.
Knowing that He is always with you;
And His grace covers you.

LORD HOW I PRAISE YOU

Lord! How I love you today
Lord! How I love you today
Oh Lord! How I love you,
Oh Lord! How I love thee
Oh Lord, how I love you today.

Jesus! I need you today
Jesus! I need you today
Oh Jesus! I need you
Oh Jesus! I need you
Oh Jesus, I need you today

Lord! How I praise you today
Lord! How I praise you today
For you always cared for me,
In your own special way,
You put angels around,
To guide me always,
Oh Lord! I give you the praise.

ASSURANCE

Come Holy Spirit, I need you.
Come Holy Spirit, I pray.
Come Holy Spirit, I need you;
Come! I need you today.

Come! With your strength and your power;
Come Holy Spirit, I pray.
Come Holy Spirit, I need you.
Come! I need you today.

Come Holy Spirit, I need you.
Come Holy Spirit, I pray.
Come! With your delivering spirit;
Come! Deliver today
Come Holy Spirit, I need you.
Come, In your own special way.

Come lay your anointing, down on me.
Lead me; help me,
So I walk your righteous way.
That I may; do your will and not mine.
Come Holy Spirit, I need you;
Come Holy Spirit I do!

Come Holy Spirit, I need you.
Come Holy Spirit, I pray.
Cleanse me! With your precious blood;

Please! Wash my sins away.
Make my burden much lighter,
That I may be able to forgive.
Come! Holy Spirit, I need you;
Come I need you, today.

Come pour in me, fill me and empower me!
Renew a right spirit within me.
So, I can bask in your presence.
That I be filled, with your precious love,
And continue to do your blessed will.

MY ENFORCER

I made you,
I molded you,
I gave you the breath of life.
I nurtured and fed you,
I paved a way for you.
I have been your anchor.
I have been your councilor.
In time of trouble,
I have uplifted you.
When times were rough,
I have been your strength,
When you were weak;
I have picked you up
When you were down
I have made the narrow road straight.
I have made the steep hills easy to climb.
I have supplied,
When there was nothing.
I have been peace
In the midst of turmoil;
I have been the calm,
In the midst of the storm;
I have been your deliverer, enforcer,
provider, and comforter.

STRENGTH

You are the center of my life,
In the midst of strife;
You are the hope,
Of my tomorrow;
That is why I love to praise your name.
You are the up- lifter in my sorrow,
When I am in doubt;
About my tomorrow;
It gives me the will, to praise your name.
When I am down,
And feel distressed,
You are the building block, of my faith;
Jesus, I will always praise your name.

AWARENESS

Look beyond the universe;
The clouds are gently floating;
Amidst is the spirit of newness.
Only take heed,
For the universe is hollow.
Jump on that floating cloud;
Accept the newness of life.
Call upon the name of Jesus!
Knowing in Him,
Your protection is constant.
With bent knees, through praise,
No matter where, or when.
Whisper a fervent prayer;
That will break issues of interruption.
For through it all,
God the Father will always be your guide.

CHRISTIAN JOURNEY

Being on this Christian journey,
It is the roughest road of all.
Storms of life get stronger;
Winds of adversity get wilder;
Our ship is tossed, from side to side.
Waves are raging,
Ship masts slumping,
Trying to weather, this stormy gale;
But an outstretch hand;
A beacon, a light;
Directs us closer, to the path of delight;
Our Master, He stands,
At the gate way to heaven!
Ready to deliver, restore and assure;
For He! Is our hope and joy
The Way, The Truth and The Light.

A FRIEND

A friend is one I can trust,
One with whom I can,
Enlighten my heart.
One who will share
My pain and sorrow;
One who will share my tomorrow!
One who will help me
Climb that difficult mountain!
One who will, move me from that valley low!
One who will guide me
Through the dark tunnel!
One who will, illuminate my light;
One who will, provide food
When I am hungry;
One who will heal my wounds;
One who will clothe me
When I am naked.
One who will help me
See the positive side of life.
One who will free me
From disgrace and confusion.
One who will be there when I am in trouble,
No matter what the situation.
One who will lay down His life for me
From entrapment and bondage;
This friend is Jesus Christ our Savior.

CONFLICTS OF LIFE

We are accused by assumptions of others
We are abused by another's false love
We are misused by what we portray
We are secluded for who we represent
We are included for our diversity
We are occluded with corruption
We are deluded because of our containment
We are deceptive through mistrust
We are rejected because of our complexity
We are hindered because of our intellect
We are manipulated to gratify others needs
We are neglected because of our shortcomings
We are afflicted by projections of others
We are persecuted for being submissive.
We are acknowledged because of our demeanor.
We are acquitted because of our noncompliance.
We are misunderstood because of our humbleness.
We should not allow ourselves to be hindered,
By what the world thinks;
We should have faith, hope and love,
Nothing else should travail.
Knowing that we have God our Father;
What more, what more, what more?

PERSEVERANCE

Put away anger and have joy.
Put away fears, show courage.
Put away hatred, let there be love.
Put away anxiety,
So you can have peace.

Grace and mercy will lift you;
Make you let go of your past.
Just recognize the present,
Persevere and move on;
No matter what the test.

Hold on to Gods' unchanging hands.
Heaven is looking down on you;
Let go, let God.
For man knows not the moment,
Or the hour that is at hand.

Just press on, in His Word
And bask in His love;
Our God, our Father, Savior from above.

HE IS A GOOD

My God! He is a good God.
My God! He is a good God.
My God! He is a good God.

He gave His son, JESUS;
Who carried my sins for me,
By dying on the cross at Calvary;
So I can be set free.

He may not come when I want Him;
But He is always on time.
He picks me up from my troubles;
Oh how I long to see His face.
He never, oh no never;
He has never, failed me yet.

In sickness and affliction;
In turmoil and distress;
In sadness and sorrow;

In pain and duress;
My Lord, my God!
He never, failed me yet.

REASSURANCE

As you fight trials,
The pains you endure.
You must then remember, Our Father!
Who abides in the heaven.
He sent His son Jesus,
Who suffered for you;

Remember my child,
Remember Him.
He died on the cross at Calvary.
The crown of thorns on His head;
The nails through His hands;
The nails through His feet;
The blood streaming, down His side;
To save your sinful lost soul;
So you my child should live and love;
That is His Father's blessings on the universe.

He arose from the dead on the third day;
So you may live life more abundantly.
Recognize what He has purposed in you;
For through His grace and mercy;
You have been redeemed.
To continue in the plan;
That he has predestined.

MY ENLIGHTENER

I am the Holy Spirit,
I am like a light;
Flickering at the end of the tunnel;
I am like a white dove;
Floating in the clouds;
I am like an angel;
Flying through the heavens;
I am not mystical, not a ghost.

I am an enlightener and an anointer.
I am the beacon for your ship.
You won't be shipwrecked or distraught;
For I will take control of your life;
I will convict you of your sins;
I will purify you,
For that's my purpose.

I will take away your doubts;
I will convince you;
Know that I am your Holy Spirit;
I am your Savior,
I am your Guide.

SUBMISSION

Whenever the load gets heavy,
Whenever the load gets light,
You can call on Him,
His name is JESUS,
He will enlighten you and make you strong.

When you are sick and cannot move,
That's when you know;
What you can prove.
That the mighty name of JESUS has power;
You just have to call on His name,
JESUS, JESUS, JESUS
And you will be healed.

Oh Jesus, the mighty name of Jesus,
Our Father, the Spirit of love.
Oh Holy Spirit; pour your anointing on me;
So I can do the work,
You have endowed me to do.

EMPOWERMENT

Believe you are powerful
Believe you are successful
Believe you are a visionary
Believe you are victorious
Believe you are a conqueror
Believe you are an achiever
Believe you are royalty
Believe you are an ambassador for Christ
Believe you are financially blessed
Believe you are economically blessed
Believe you are spiritually blessed
For without thinking; with no doubt
Most of all, believe who and whose you are,
A child of the king
The Father in heaven who knows your purpose

ACKNOWLEDGEMENT

Always remember
To praise and worship him daily,
Read your bible daily,
It is the food of life.
Start off with five minutes,
Better than zero.
There is no luck,
But there is faith,
Love and obedience,
In a believers life,
To be prosperous
So be thoughtful,
Thankful and forever grateful

DISCERNMENT

I was walking down the street,
Problem came by to indulge.
Happiness came by with joy,
Then pushed problem away,
Love overpowered them and brought faith along;
Faith played no games and brought in the Holy Spirit;
This then exacerbated!
They altogether pulled down strongholds.
This motivated me, to be thankful and grateful.
This left a constant glow over me; which has been inexplicable.

BLESSED FRUITS

There was a spirit which was beyond control
Then suddenly Peace came in;
The atmosphere became calm
All hearts got full of joy.
Loving kindness and happiness,
As they gather at the pond,
Where the spirit of tranquility flows
God our Father, is the only one who knows,
All our inner thoughts and our being.

GOD IS

Praise and worship Him daily;
You are blessed through God,
Who is the giver of life.
Without God there is no way out,
Always remember,
No matter what you may attain;
Whichever heights you climb;
God is in charge.
He is the one who sustains,
He is the only provider,
He is the first the head of your life always.

LIFE

We can be egoistic about life as a whole,
A small yet big word,
We can define that word Life in many ways;
Life is great,
It is what we make of it,
How we perceive it,
How we live it,
Being able to endure, the bumps along the way,
As we look back and reflect;
Not pondering on the past;
But using our experiences,
As a tool for greater achievements.

WHAT IS LIFE

L – Living, loving, seeing each other in the form of beauty
I – Igniting ones' heart with peace through prayer
F – Fearless of the unknown
E – Escalating beyond our endeavors

WHY WE LIVE

L – Live vibrantly
I – Inspire everyone with love and hope
V- View each other as our equal and not less than
E – Evangelize to the world about Jesus Christ our Savior

PURPOSE

God gave us life to live abundantly
To follow in His footsteps,
By being Christ –like, caring, giving, sharing
Compassionate and not critical of each other
But see each brother and sister as angels
As our Father in heaven looks upon us

POSITIVE ATTRIBUTES

Think positive
Act positive
Live positive
The ability to be successful,
Derives from these focuses
Being faithful and prayerful
Also having a positive attitude
Will help you achieve your goals productively in life

THOUGHTFULNESS

Lord we falter and sin,
We shed a tear and sigh,
Fearful and distraught,
Though we know you are near.
Our burdens you bear,
For on you we can rely,
As we go from day to day,
You will never turn us away.
Through your grace and your mercy,
Your love and compassion,
We know that you are
Our comforting Savior

THANKFULNESS

Lord we thank you
For the breath of life;
We thank you for your caring,
We thank you for your guidance
And your precious divine love.

QUIET MOMENT

Be still and listen
Obedient and submissive,
In the quiet of the moment
You will hear the Lord speak;
For you will receive discernment,
To know what He has called you to do
As you are blessed to be a blessing in others life.

BLESSINGS

The lord blesses you,
He gives you peace and joy,
Bountiful blessings He will give
More than you can contain.
Through troubles and trials,
Through sorrow and pain,
He will never leave nor forsake you,
He will be with you always
Even until the end.

WHO HAS IT

God has the glory
Boys and girls have the power,
I have the power,
You have the power,
We all have the power,
The power has us,
That's the Holy Ghost power
And it's inside of us.

DIVINE INTIMACY

Let the joy of the Lord be upon you
The peace of the Lord be with you
The glory of the Lord be all over you
That you be filled with the spirit of love
So that the holy spirit infill you
And edify your soul

INFILL ME

Bridging heaven and earth
Truthfulness and faithfulness are inclusive
To instill in us the word
Transform our hearts
Unite us as one as effervescent love overflows
So that we can attain spiritual manifestation

DIRECTION

It is a good life
With tough situations
The bitter and the sweet
The rough and the smooth
The real world it is not easy
There are rough hills and rocky roads
But if you keep God on your side
And you work hard to keep the faith
Any goal can be achieved
Always stay focused
Keep positive people around you
The sky is the limit,
Make high goals for yourself
Have big dreams and follow them
Take care of your responsibility effectively
Make an effort until
You become productive
In the way God has purposed
Then success will be your uttermost goal
And your endeavor will not be in vain

AFTERMATH

Disaster strikes and hurt is left
Turmoil then transcends
Pain and fear is succumbed
Amidst the lost and forgotten trail
There is a God, a comforter, a healer
A peacemaker who calms it all
And delivers us from this ruthlessness
He gives us love
He gives us care
He gives us what we fear to share
The Bible, the Word, the Gospel, the Truth
He understands
He makes a way
For he is the one
Who gave us abundant life
We are transformed
From above and below
Across and beyond
Our thoughts flow
Our minds sway
Then our imagination becomes real
Through him comes manifestation
Then our thoughts become clarified
And we are then edified

ENDURANCE

God blesses
His love comforts
His spirit flows through
A moment of laughter
A moment of cheer
Through sickness and health
Through sorrow and pain
A friendship to cherish
From now till the end

OBEDIENCE

Wait and be still
You listen
You will hear
You are called
Don't be obstinate
Lay low and do not react
Did you do what you were asked?
Or just what you wanted
What you were advised
Or what you decided
Be cautious, do right
Obey and follow
The direction and the path
You were purposed by God

HOPE

If I have hope I know I have help
I am capable of doing all things
Through Christ who strengthens me
With God nothing is impossible
Because of Jesus Christ
I am confident
That I can respond to anything
With knowledge and information
From events and challenges
I have experienced in my life
And move on to the higher calling
For which God has called me to be

GRATEFULNESS

I wake up each day
Knowing God has blessed me
Looking out of the window pane
At the beauty of His creation
There are no issues to withhold
There is no sorrow
That cannot be controlled
For the master he said
I will take care of you
I know the Lord has a purpose
For each one of us
And if only I stay focused
Stand solely on His word
There is nothing through Jesus
Too great or too small
Nothing through Him
That I cannot endure

THE CROSS

As I gaze upon the cross
That stands upon the hill
I reflect upon the crucifixion
Knowing how He gave his life for me
I know I do not deserve
What he did for me
His love, his grace, his mercy
Was totally beyond compare
Knowing the purpose for his suffering
Was to deliver me from sin
This was all for my sins
So I could be set free
He lay in the tomb
Three days then He arose
For me to realize
The purpose of his sacrifice
He did not have to do it
But through obedience to his
Father He was sent to do this mission
This he did submissively

VICTORY

Lord, I know you died for me
Lord you died on the cross at Calvary
Oh Lord, oh Lord
You did this all to deliver me

Lord I know that I am free
Oh Lord, I know you lifted me
Oh Lord my Savior
Who saved me

Lord I know I am healed Lord
I know you touched my soul
Lord, oh Lord, you are the one
Who shed your blood for me

Lord you saved my soul
From sin, grief and sadness
Oh Lord my God all this you did for me

Lord I am praying as you mold me
Lord I am praising as you use me
I am asking you to keep me
Lord please teach me,
Reach me, touch my soul
For my desire is to do your will

GLORY TO GOD

Glory, glory, hallelujah
Glory, glory, I give you the praise

You are worthy
You are worthy
Hallelujah, I give you the praise

You're a deliverer
You're a deliverer
Hallelujah, I give you the praise

You are mighty
You are mighty
Hallelujah, I give you the praise

You are a conqueror
You are a conqueror
Hallelujah, I give you the praise

PEACE

The spirit of the Lord is in you
This lets your glory shine
The love of the Lord is in you
That give you joy divine
May the anointing flow
From within and throughout
Your family and your home
Let the river of peace continually flow
In the community where you live
As the Lord has graced you
To evangelize His Word

PRAISE TO GOD

Thank you Jesus
Thank you Jesus
Thank you Jesus
I give you the praise

I shout for joy Lord
I shout for joy Lord
I clap my hands Lord
And give you the praise

I lift my heart Lord
I stomp my feet Lord
I jump for joy Lord
Hallelujah, I give you the praise
Hallelujah, hallelujah, hallelujah
I give you the praise

PERSEVERANCE

We wonder we ponder
In our storm and distress
Why we ask and say Lord Jesus
Lift us up to our Father
The glory of our life
Every heartache and pain
The sorrow and duress
In our everyday life
Will eventually pass away
For it is all but a test
So we have to do our best
Though loved ones are gone
We will remember always
For they were once ours
But we give them back to Our Father
Which art in heaven
To whom they belong
As He goes to prepare a place
Where they can abide with Him
And accompany the angels
As they joyfully sing

THE COMFORTER

No matter what you're going through
You have Jesus there to comfort you
Don't you worry for surely you'll be happy
With assurance there is someone on the main line
Who knows and sees your every need

When in doubt just give a shout
For there is someone by the name of Jesus
Who is there to pull you out
Don't you worry don't you fear
For there is our God who is always there

Yesterday is gone, today is promised
Tomorrow is not here, but is envisioned
Take one day at a time
And keep your thoughts focused
On the one who gave you life
The one and only Creator
God the Father Almighty

CHOSEN

I was called, appointed, anointed
Chosen by God
Sent to deliver
The message of love
Of a man Christ the King

Born in a lowly manger
Died on a cross at Calvary
Arose from death in a tomb where he lay
On the third day and lived

To redeem and have us set free
Healing salvation and deliverance
This is His plan for His people
Yes the story has and is still being told

BLESSINGS

I rise in the morning
I look up and praise our Lord for another day
I don't just look up
To almighty God for help
When I am troubled and distressed
I look and see the beauty of the skies

The birds with their melodious chirping that give us joy
The rainbow of many colors that give us hope
The ray of sunshine that give happiness
The flowers in their splendor to show us glory
The animals with their caring to show us love
The universe to give us peace
The stars in the sky to give us comfort

I will forgive repent put away the past
So the grey clouds can be removed
And I can see the silver lining
I will let go of the past and deal with the present
I won't step back but put one step forward
I look up and I'm grateful to our Creator
For the beauty of His work

Look up to the hills from where comes my help
Ask God forgiveness
For the wrong things I do
Be thankful look up and move on
Thank God for the work He has done

DESOLATE

In my lonely room
In my time of gloom
I look around and ask is this a tomb
At sunrise, at sunset, and dusk
I pause and I ponder
Then rescind my question
I gaze at the ceiling
I see magnificent visions of angels
It is then I realize this room is my own
The gloom I had no more
It was in this room that I received
The wisdom from above
Glory be to God
The one who showed me love

ESSENCE

When I was sick,
When I was troubled
When I was lonely,
When I was lost
Jesus you were there
Above, around and beside me
I am your child in your image and likeness
The one for who you shed your blood
To set free from sin

Yours from dust to being
Yours from heart to heart
Yours from breast to breast
Yours from the womb to the earth
Yours when I leave this body
Yours when my soul leaves to be
With you in eternity

I will praise you
I will magnify you
Your name is Jesus
The Lord of Lords
The King of Kings
The Prince of Peace
The bright and morning star
Lord I will always love you
For your comfort and your care

SERENITY

Oh give thanks unto the Lord
For all he has done
The joy he has instilled in me
With His spirit He infills me
The anointing he has endowed on me
I bless Him for His serenity

I WAS LOST
I was lost but I was found In the midst of my confusion
I had to stop in desperation
And come to a conclusion
That the free will which was given
Was to serve my God of heaven
And not the man on earth

LIGHTHOUSE

It is so assuring
To look back and see
How we impact the life of others
In all we say and do
And the energy we can release
To help one come through
The power God has infused in us
The plan He has for us
To use us as His lighthouse
To help empower each other
To direct them to a place of purpose
He has predestined for us
For the Lord has already done His work

THE REDEEMER

Jesus is the shepherd
The Savior, the Redeemer
He carried the cross
Climbed the hills of Crux
Was crucified and died
On the cross at Calvary
So His people be saved and set free

For I was blind
A sin sick soul
I could not see
The suffering He endured
To save a wretch like me
To heal me from my hurt and pain
That's what He did to set me free

MOTHER

Mother who is kind, loving and caring
Giving and sharing without reservation
Willing and able to listen and confer
Mother who shed tears of joy and sorrow
Went down on her knees in the midst of an uproar
Mother, she is forgiving holds no remorse
For she just allowed things to run its course
She let nothing hinder her
From the vision God has given her
For the mission she is going to complete
To do her masters will

GRACE

Amazing and abounding grace
For which I am not deserving
Has freed me from the debts of sin
So I can be restored
Redeemed me from a debt I owe
That I can never repay
Exempted me from eternal death
And gained eternal life

DON'T BE DISMAYED

Don't get disappointed
Don't let your countenance fail
For in the midst of all confusion
There is no room for discouragement
There is a God who keeps appointments
And He knows your every disappointment
So do not be dismayed whatever betide
Know that there is one
Only in Him you can confide
Lord your God He will always be at your side

COURAGE

Do not look at my shell
See within me
Look beyond my age
And see my courage
Though you may not be aware
To what I have had to bear
I would like to you show
Maybe what you already know
I am a woman of distinction Me!
I have no conviction
Do not reflect on my pain
For I see my aim
For I have Jesus Christ
Through Him I will suffice
The world and its demise

MY ENFORCER

When I awoke in the midst of the night
I felt a new feeling come upon me
Not from my own delight
But through Gods power and might
He enlightened me
He ignited me
He empowered me
For I opened my heart
From the plight for the mission with
Our Savior, deliverer, redeemer
The Lord Jesus Christ our king

CONVICTION

Open my eye so I can see
What the Lord has done for me
He carried the cross for me you see
Was nailed on it for me at Calvary
My sins for me He did atone
As his blood was shed to set me free

BECAUSE OF WHO YOU ARE

Come into my life
Come into my life
Come into my life Lord Jesus

Come in today come in today
Come in to stay
Come into my life Lord Jesus

Holy, Holy, Holy Lord
Holy, precious, divine Lord
Come into my life I need you
Come into my life to stay

Father, Son and Holy Ghost
You are the one I love the most
I lift up praises to you
You are my guide in what I do

You are the only one I have
In the midst of turmoil
The only hope I have is you God the Father
When I praise and glorify your name
When I kneel and magnify your word
My blessings just come flowing through

THANK YOU LORD

I say thank you Lord
When my burden is heavy
And don't know where to turn
I still say thank you Lord

I say thank you Lord
The mountain is so high
I don't know how to climb
I say thank you Lord

I say thank you Lord
The valley is so low
I don't know where to go
I say thank you Lord

I say thank you Lord
The way is so narrow
But I will still follow
And say thank you Lord

You picked me up and turned me around
Placed my feet on solid ground
No matter what the test may be
I'll praise and say thank you Lord

I say thank you Lord You paved the way
I'll stay the course and follow your path
Praise and glorify your name
Say hallelujah, I thank you Lord

FAMILY AND FRIENDS

Can we stand firm and care for each other
Can we bear each other's pain?
Can we forgive and move on?
Can we accept and respect each other?
Can we love from the heart and not the mouth?
Can we care by giving willingly?
Not for self recognition or self gratification
Can we be receptive of others and not deceptive?

For if we are family or friend
We will have nicks and bends
But let us not belittle
Let us not envy
Let us not hate
Let us not separate
Let us not distinguish
Let us relinquish
Things of the past
Let us not be separated
Let us not be selfish
For united we stand
Divided we fall
Also remember when the good Lord calls
We through the same door will go
The blood in our veins color's the same
We ought to remember we're in the same race

When we have been laid to rest
The dust we once were we will return
The ashes and remnants will all be the same
So live life happily
Abide in unity

Embrace each other
Through our faith and sincere Christian love
And glorify our Father in heaven above

THE LORD IS MY SHEPHERD

(translated)
The Lord is my guide, keeper, rock, shelter

Why should I worry?
He supplies all my needs

He has paved the way, he has fed me
He took me to a place of serenity
He gave me peace

He leads me in the right direction
To a safe haven in His care

Yes though I go through trials, tribulations
storms and warfare
I will not worry about the adversities or adversaries
My Savior is with me always
He places a hedge of protection around me
Has His angel to watch over me
And His Holy Spirit to guide me to a place of safety

You provide for me
In the eyes of the unbelievers
Even while every storm is raging

You have empowered me
You have filled me with uprightness
Until I am overflowing with joy

After You brought me through the storm and trials of life
You fed me, gave me peace, joy and happiness
And took me to a place of comfort and safety
Knowing that by Your grace and mercy
You brought me through all this

I will always remember
What You did for me
Why should I turn away?
Why should I go back to my old ways?
Knowing what You Jesus have done for me
Remembering this transformation
I should be able to stand
The test of time on this planet earth
Until I join up with Him in the spirit
Where I will live forever in His house

THE LORD IS MY SHEPHERD
PSALM 23

The Lord is my Shepherd
I shall not want
He makes me to lie down in green pastures
He leads me besides still waters
He restores my soul
He leads me in the path of righteousness
For His names sake

Yea, though I walk through the valley of the
Shadow of death, I will fear no evil
For You are with me Your rod and Your staff
They comfort me
You prepare a table before me in the presence of my enemies
You anoint my head with oil my cup runeth over
Surely goodness and mercy
Shall follow me all the days of my life
And I will dwell in the house of the Lord forever

BIOGRAPHY

I was born in Curacao, Netherlands, Antilles. I lived in Castries, St. Lucia, until the age of 20, when I moved to London, England. I graduated from St. Hillier Hospital Nursing School, Carshalton, Surrey as a Licensed Practical Nurse; and Milford Chest Hospital, Godalming, Surrey England as a Thoracic Nurse. I then moved to U.S.A. in 1979 where I continued with my nursing career. I earned my GED tutoring while my kids were in afterschool program; graduated in June 1986 with my GED. In January 2008 I graduated from the 25TH class of the Suffolk County Citizen's Police Academy, where I proudly belong to the Alumni Association. After 29years of residing in New York, I then decided to apply for USA citizenship status which I received in August 2008. Graduated from Grace Bible Institute, Humble Texas, with Certificate in Christian Counseling, October 2008.I also graduated from New York Theological Seminary with Certificate in Christian Ministry in May 2010. I am a proud blessed mother of three lovely children, and seven beautiful grand children. I am a believer who knows that God will give me wisdom, knowledge and understanding; and He will inspire me in what He has predestined for me if I only be still, open my heart and be receptive to that voice.

I received the inspiration to write while recovering from a stroke in 1999; I enjoy reading, writing, and listening to music especially jazz, classical and gospel.

ACKNOWLEDGEMENT

I give glory and honor to God my Father who has inspired me in all aspects of my life even when the going was tough.

Bibles used: KJB; NLT; NKJ; NSB for permission of scriptures and quotations used.

To my mother who did not know about my writing but encouraged me, before she passed and went to meet her maker, telling me God has greater things for me to do.

To my children Jillian, Nicole, and Shaun.

My friends Sylvia and Eric who has been my support in critical situations, and helped motivate me. Mother Banks who gave counsel and support when I lost my Mom, Sandra Green my sister in Christ who was there in testing times, Sister Anita Turner helped with my editing; Sis Geraldine Griggs my encourager; Professor Scottie Owens who had faith in me Bro. Slaughter, Bro Chue my brothers in Christ who attended church with me and encourage me to read poems at programs; etching me on to pursue my writing.

Dedicate to my Grandmother Martha Inglis who has always been my strength.
To all Gods' children who has been supportive to me spiritually with encouraging words of wisdom.